This book belongs to:

_____

It was given to me by:

_____

On:

_____

Bible
Devotions
for Bedtime

BARBOUR
PUBLISHING

Published by Barbour Publishing, Inc., P.O. Box 719, Uhrichsville, Ohio 44683, www.barbourbooks.com

Our mission is to publish and distribute inspirational products offering exceptional value and biblical encouragement to the masses.

 Member of the
Evangelical Christian
Publishers Association

Printed in China.

Bible
Devotions
for Bedtime

DANIEL PARTNER
ILLUSTRATED BY RICHARD HOIT

Table of Contents

"In the beginning
God. . ."

In the beginning God
created the heavens
and the earth.

Genesis 1:1

When you read a book, it is
important to know what that book is
about. This is not hard to do. Sometimes
the name of the book tells you. The
book called *The Cat in the Hat* is about a
cat wearing a hat. There is a book called
The Adventures of Peter Rabbit. It is a
book about exciting things that happen
to a rabbit named Peter. And the name
The Cat in the Hat Comes Back tells you
just what that book is about.

What do you think the Bible is

about? The word *bible* means "book." That name doesn't give a hint about what's inside the book. But read the first four words of the Bible: "In the beginning God. . ." Do these words tell you what the Bible is about? Yes! The Bible is about God.

True, the Bible tells about many things and many people. But all in all, the Bible is meant to show you who God is and what God has done for you.

Dear God

Thank You for the Bible,
which tells me all about You.

"Let bright
lights appear."

And God said, "Let bright lights appear in the sky."

Genesis 1:14

It is good that the sky is not empty. How boring that would be! All day long, we would see only blue sky. And at night, we would see nothing but black. God wanted more than this. So the Bible says, "God made two great lights, the sun and the moon, to shine down upon the earth. The greater one, the sun, presides during the day; the lesser one, the moon, presides through the night. He also made the stars."

The greater light rules the day. What is that light? It is the sun. The lesser light rules the night. What do you think this is? That's easy! It is the moon. And God made the stars, too.

On the first day there was light. But God wanted more than just that light. So He made the sun and moon and stars on the fourth day. You may be able to think of some reasons for these lights in the sky. They're very pretty, aren't they? The sunshine is so warm, and it makes things grow.

The Bible gives reasons for the sun, moon, and stars. It says that the sun divides the day from the night. The changing shape of the moon and patterns of the stars are sometimes helpful, kind of like road signs. And all three mark the changing seasons, days, and years. God said this was good. Don't you think so, too?

Dear God

Thank You for the sun, the moon, and the stars.

"So God
created. . ."

So God created great sea creatures and every sort of fish and every kind of bird. . . . God made all sorts of wild animals, livestock, and small animals.

Genesis 1:21, 25

Do you like animals? If you answered yes, that's great! Because on the fifth day, God made the waters swarm with fish and other life. And the skies were filled with birds of every kind. God created big sea creatures, too. Think about all the different kinds of birds and fish there are. God made each one! God saw that this was good and blessed them all.

Wait, there's more!

The next day, God decided that there should be all kinds of other animals. So God made livestock like cattle, sheep, and goats. He made small animals and other wildlife. Plus, He made all the things that creep on the ground, like bugs and snakes and lizards.

Just about everything was made by this time, right? There was earth and sky and sea. The sun, moon, and stars were shining bright. Plants and trees and grass grew fresh and green. And there were animals everywhere, on land and in the sea and sky.

Could anything be missing? Think

about it. . . . Yes, something is missing. You aren't there! There are no people yet. That's coming up next!

Dear God

I love the animals that You made— thank You for all of them!

" . . .masters
over all life."

Then God said, "Let us make people in our image, to be like ourselves. They will be masters over all life."

Genesis 1:26

What do you see when you look out your window? I see the blue sky peeking through a tree's branches and leaves. The tree grows on a low slope covered with different kinds of bushes, grasses, and plants. Everything is shades of green. Some purple flowers bloom on a bush. A golden hummingbird visits little orange flowers scattered here and there. Yellow bees buzz by. Sometimes a big black dragonfly flies in and stops in midair. The sunshine makes shadows. The breeze from the ocean makes them jiggle and shake. A silvery spider's web shimmers in the window frame.

God made all this and more, more than anyone can even imagine! Have you ever thought about why the heavens and the earth are here? Why is the earth covered with living things? Here's why: God worked for the first five days of Creation to get ready for the sixth day. That is the day God made people.

Remember the taste of your favorite food and the smell you like the best. Imagine the softest thing you know—a kitten's fur, a feather, the petal of a flower. God made these and all things just for you!

Dear God

Thank You for everything I can see, hear, smell, and touch.

"God rested."

On the seventh day,
having finished his task,
God rested from all
his work.
Genesis 2:2

The Bible tells about God's power. And God is strong, too. But God is much more than powerful and strong. God is also holy, eternal, faithful, wise, true, and good. God is light. God is love. God is so much that there are not enough words to tell it all!

The Bible is the book that tells us all we need to know about God. The first thing it says is that God is the Creator, and it tells the story of

Creation. And there are not just six days in the Creation story. It took God seven days to finish making everything. The first six days were for working. Then on the seventh day, God rested from all His work. First, God worked to create everything. What is the second thing the Bible tells about God? It says that God rested. But God is so strong and powerful. Why would He need to rest? Maybe to help us remember that we should take time to rest, too!

Dear God

Thank You for being who You are—powerful, holy, and full of love.

"And the LORD
God formed. . ."

And the LORD God formed
a man's body from the dust
of the ground and breathed
into it the breath of life.
And the man became
a living person.

Genesis 2:7

This verse gives us a lot to think
about. It tells about how people came to
be here. First, it says that God formed us.
All the other creatures were created and
made. But we human beings were
formed.

Have you ever formed something
out of clay? You soften the clay with the

warmth of your hands. You roll it or cut it. You shape it and reshape it. You work with the clay until it becomes what you want it to be.

People were to be different from the rest of Creation. This is why the Bible uses a new word to describe how we came to be. It says, "God formed man." It didn't happen fast. God worked step-by-step and was very careful when He made us. This shows how important we are in God's plan. God worked to make us right and beautiful. Another part of the Bible says, "Lord, you are our Father. We are the clay, and you are the potter. We are all formed by your hand."

Dear God

Thank You for taking the time to make me special.

"...and there he placed the man."

Then the LORD God
planted a garden in Eden,
in the east, and there
he placed the man
he had created.

Genesis 2:8

The first people God created were named Adam and Eve. They lived in a garden in Eden. This was a huge place. All the animals were there; trees and plants were growing; and rivers were flowing. Gold and precious stones were there. It must have been more beautiful than anything we've ever seen!

There God brought the animals

and birds to the first man. Adam gave them all names. Imagine that! Adam was so smart that he could give a different name to every animal. He knew each and every one. Adam cared for the garden by working as a farmer. And it was there in the garden that God made the woman, Eve. The two were married in the garden at Eden.

If you like animals, you would have liked that garden. If you like flowers and trees, Eden was the place for you. What would you do there? You could swim in the rivers. You could collect precious stones. You could climb trees. You could plant and grow things. You could live with the animals.

All these things are wonderful. But they are not what really made Eden so wonderful. Here is why Eden was so good: God walked there in the cool evenings. He spoke to Adam and Eve, and they talked to Him. God was there, so it was paradise!

Dear God

Thank You for our planet, but most of all for Your presence.

"Adam chose a
name for
each one."

So the Lord God formed from the soil every kind of animal and bird. He brought them to Adam to see what he would call them, and Adam chose a name for each one.

Genesis 2:19

Do you know someone who you think is smart? This could be your mother or father, or a family member. Certainly, your schoolteacher knows a lot more than you do. But Adam was very smart. God brought all the animals to him. Then Adam chose a name for each one. Think of the names of as many animals as you can. How many animal names do you know? How many animal names does your father or mother know? How about your teacher?

Adam didn't just know every animal name, he is the one who gave all the animals their names! This means that he named every farm animal, every bird, and every wild animal. Adam probably named all the bugs and fish, too. This shows that God made people to be very, very smart!

Dear God

Thank You for making me
so smart!

"I will make
a companion."

And the LORD God said,
"It is not good for the man
to be alone. I will make
a companion
who will help him."
Genesis 2:18

The very first man was all alone in that great big garden. God knew this, and He cared that Adam was alone. So God made all the animals and brought them to Adam. Was this how God wanted to fill Adam's loneliness? Were the animals to be Adam's companions on this earth?

Adam must have looked at each

animal very carefully. After all, he gave each one a name. Giraffe, pig, alligator, dog, cat, elephant. How many kinds of animals are there? Tens of thousands, maybe millions. Adam knew them all. But after he had given them each a name, he was still alone. Adam still did not have a wife, someone to be his friend and helper in life.

There were so many wonderful animals. Adam must have enjoyed them. But no animal was right to be Adam's lifelong mate. What would you do to keep Adam from being alone? God did one final thing in order to complete the Creation. God made a woman.

Dear God

Thank You for making
a helper for Adam.

"God made
a woman."

So the LORD God caused Adam to fall into a deep sleep. He took one of Adam's ribs. . . . Then the LORD God made a woman from the rib and brought her to Adam.

Genesis 2:21–22

Think of all that God did to make the heavens and the earth. When God spoke the word, there was light and day and night, the sky and the dry land and the sea. When God spoke, the sun, moon, and stars appeared in the sky. Over and over again Genesis tells us, "And God said." That's how the Creation appeared—grass, herbs, and trees; fish and birds and even huge whales. All this happened because God spoke!

Then God changed the way of Creation. "And the Lord God formed a man's body from the dust of the ground and breathed into it the breath of life. And the man became a living person." God didn't just speak to make Adam. God worked to form him from dust. Then, so that Adam would have life, God breathed into him.

But Adam could not be alone. He needed a mate, someone who matched him in every way. This is why God made woman in a new and different way. God didn't speak or use dust, like before. Unlike everything else, woman was made from a part of Adam. And Adam said, "She is part of my own flesh and bone! She will be called 'woman,' because she was taken out of a man."

Dear God

Thank You for giving the breath of life to Adam—and to me!

". . .he asked
the woman."

Now the serpent was the shrewdest of all the creatures the LORD God had made. "Really?" he asked the woman. "Did God really say you must not eat any of the fruit in the garden?"

Genesis 3:1

The Bible is full of stories. Many of these are about good people who do good things. Bible stories tell of brave men and women and of people with courage and love. The Bible also tells stories of what God has done and will do for us.

But the Bible tells some sad stories, too. The saddest story tells how Adam and Eve failed God. It shows them leaving the wonderful Garden of Eden. We see them here for the first time living without God. This is the worst thing that could happen to them and to us.

There were many different kinds of trees in the garden. God said that the man and woman could eat the fruit of all those trees except for one—the tree of the knowledge of good and evil. This seems simple, doesn't it? But a powerful enemy of God entered Eden looking like a snake. This snake asked Eve which trees she could eat fruit from. It was a simple question, and Eve knew the right answer. But the snake tempted Eve to eat the forbidden fruit anyway, and this was the beginning of the fall of humanity into sin. Soon our simple, beautiful life with God would end.

Dear God

Help me to do what makes You happy— help me to do what is right.

"She ate some of the fruit."

So she ate some of the fruit. She also gave some to her husband, who was with her. Then he ate it, too.

Genesis 3:6

A terrible thing happened when Adam and Eve ate the fruit of the only tree that God told them not to eat from. The people of the Garden of Eden died! God said this would happen if they ate of that tree. And it did happen.

It may not seem to you that they died. After all, they didn't drop dead after eating the fruit. Since this is true, it teaches that there are two kinds of death. One comes when our body dies. When our body is dead, we cannot live in this world anymore. But this is not what happened to Adam and Eve. After they ate the fruit, they knew their bodies were naked, and so they made clothes out of leaves. So we know they were still alive in their bodies.

But there is another kind of death.

Think of pretty flowers in a vase. They have all their color, and they may even smell good. They seem to be alive, but they are not. These flowers have been cut off from their roots in the soil. They can't get their food from the earth anymore. In time, they will wilt away. In fact, they are already dead.

In the same way, Adam and Eve were cut off from God. That's what God meant when He said they would die if they ate the forbidden fruit.

Dear God

Teach me to be
alive in You—
to trust
what You say.

"...the tree
of life."

After banishing them from the garden, the LORD God stationed mighty angelic beings to the east of Eden. And a flaming sword flashed back and forth, guarding the way to the tree of life.

Genesis 3:24

There was another important tree in the Garden of Eden. To understand the Bible, you must know about this tree. It is the tree of life.

Adam and Eve could have chosen to eat from the tree of life. Instead, they ate from the tree of the knowledge of good and evil. So they died by losing their link with God. This sin also brought death to their bodies. If they had eaten from the tree of life, every-thing would be different today. There would be no death. We would all be living with God. Everyone would have eternal life.

The way to the tree of life was cut off because Adam sinned. Then there was no way for people to have eternal life. It is a sad story, but there is good news! God did not forget us when Adam sinned. Later, He sent Jesus Christ into the world to show us the way to eternal life. So, don't be sad. Believe in Jesus and the way to the tree of life will open to you!

Dear God

Thank You for sending Your son, Jesus, for me!

"It broke
his heart."

And he saw that all their thoughts were consistently and totally evil. So the LORD was sorry he had ever made them.
It broke his heart.

Genesis 6:5–6

The journey from Genesis chapter three to chapter six is not happy. But in chapter six, things get better. This chapter tells of Noah and the ark—a good story about how God solved the problem of man's wickedness. God saw how bad the people on the earth were, and He was sorry that He had made them. So

He decided to destroy every living creature on the earth. "I'll wipe out people, animals, birds, and reptiles," said God.

The bright spot in this story is Noah. He was the only person who lived right and obeyed God. Everyone else, the Bible says, was terribly cruel and violent.

So God told Noah, "Get some wood and build a boat."

You may know how the rest of the story goes. The boat that Noah built was Noah's ark. Noah, his family, and animals of every kind went into the ark. Then it began to rain. It didn't stop raining for forty days! The flood destroyed everything except for what was in the ark. In the end, Noah and his family began a new world.

God judged the human race in Noah's time. He destroyed everything. But in the ark, God made a way of escape. For us today, that way is Jesus Christ.

Dear God

Thank You for sending Jesus Christ to save people in this world.

". . .safe
in the boat."

"Look! I am about to cover the earth with a flood that will destroy every living thing. Everything on earth will die! But I solemnly swear to keep you safe in the boat, with your wife and your sons and their wives."

Genesis 6:17–18

Have you ever seen a picture of Noah leading animals into the ark? This may be the most pictured event in the Bible. You've probably seen it in books. It is also on puzzles, posters, wallpaper, blankets, curtains, and bed sheets. There are Noah's ark mobiles to hang in baby cribs. There are Noah's ark plush toys to line up on your bed. Could there be any child in America who hasn't seen a picture of Noah's ark?

It is good that people see pictures of Noah and the ark. Noah is usually shown with a long white beard. His wife is at his side, and they both wear long robes. Animals line up in twos, waiting to go into the ark. Usually giraffes, elephants, and lions are there along with some smaller animals. The ark is huge! It looks strong and well built. It has to be so that it can float above God's terrible watery judgment on the earth.

Pictures of Noah's ark remind us that God wants to rescue everyone from judgment. Jesus Christ is like the ark—strong and safe. When you believe in Him, it is like entering the ark. In Him, you are safe from judgment.

Dear God

Thank You for keeping us safe when we believe in You.

"Noah, his wife,
and his sons. . ."

So Noah, his wife, and his sons and their wives left the boat. . . . Then Noah built an altar to the LORD.
Genesis 8:18, 20

Noah was six hundred years old when he went into the ark to escape the flood. All his family went inside, too. The water in the earth started gushing out everywhere. The sky opened like a window, and rain poured down for forty days and nights. The water became deeper and deeper until the boat could float.

The flood became so deep that even the highest mountains were under water! Not an animal or person was left alive anywhere on the earth. Nothing was alive except Noah and his family and the animals in the ark.

One hundred fifty days later, God made a wind blow. The rain stopped and the flooding stopped. One day the ark came to rest on a mountain. After a while, the other mountaintops could be seen. Finally, the earth was dry. Then God said, "You may now leave the ark." After Noah's family had gone out of the boat, the animals all left, too.

What a terrible time that must have been! And when it was all over, what was the first thing Noah did? He worshiped God. Noah is your example. He teaches you that no matter what happens, remember to worship God.

Dear God

Help me to remember to worship You— no matter what happens in my life.

"I am giving
you a sign."

And God said, "I am giving you a sign. . . . I have placed my rainbow in the clouds. . . . Never again will there be a flood that will destroy all life."

Genesis 9:12–13, 15

Do you like to see a rainbow in the sky? They are so beautiful! Do you know what makes a rainbow? Sun shining through falling rain. But in Noah's time, there had never been a rainbow before. The rains that brought the flood were the first rains ever. When Noah saw the rains ending, the sun came out. Then

Noah and his family saw the very first rainbow ever, and they knew they had survived the Great Flood.

Imagine what Noah's family felt the next time rain clouds came. They must have been afraid of the rain. After all, the first time it rained, the flood destroyed the whole earth! But God didn't want them to be afraid. God promised Noah and his family that He would never again destroy the earth with a flood. Rainbows are a reminder that this promise is true. God has kept this promise to Noah. Since the time of Noah, floods have never destroyed the whole earth. Remember this whenever you see a rainbow.

The Bible tells many of God's promises. All these are as real and beautiful as a rainbow. And all of them are true!

Dear God

Thank You for always keeping Your word!

"The Lord guided them."

The LORD guided them
by a pillar of cloud during
the day and a pillar of
fire at night.
Exodus 13:21

When the children of Israel
escaped Egypt, they knew exactly which
way to go. The Lord guided them day
and night. During the day, they followed
a pillar of cloud. At night, it became a
pillar of fire. This pillar may have looked
like a huge pine tree that was made out
of cloud and fire.

Even though they knew God was
leading them, the Israelites were often
afraid and tired of their journey. Once

they came to a place called Rephidim. There was no water there, so they complained to Moses, "Give us water to drink!" They were sorry they'd ever left Egypt and thought that they would die.

Moses didn't know what to do. "What should I do with these people?" he cried to God. "They are about to stone me!"

"Take your shepherd's staff and walk ahead of the people," the Lord answered. "I'll meet you by the rock at Mount Sinai. Strike the rock, and water will come pouring out." Sure enough, water gushed out of the rock.

Today, Jesus Christ is like that rock. He provides the water that we need to never be thirsty again. He said, "But the water I give them takes away thirst altogether. It becomes a perpetual spring within them, giving them eternal life."

Dear God

Thank You for Your son, Jesus, who gives us eternal life.

"Let me go out
into the fields."

One day Ruth said to Naomi, "Let me go out into the fields to gather leftover grain behind anyone who will let me do it."

Ruth 2:2

Ruth was very poor. You can see this in the way she got her food. She gleaned behind the reapers—the people who cut grain used to make bread. To glean means to gather up the leftovers. In those days, reapers left some grain at the edges of the fields. Some grain dropped along the way. A gleaner picked up this unwanted grain. Today, some very poor people search through dumpsters for food that has been thrown away. They could also be called gleaners.

Poor Ruth. She was young and unwanted. Her husband was dead, and she ate what others didn't want. She had only one thing going for her. She had attached herself to Naomi—a child of Israel and a believer in God.

Naomi was the mother of Ruth's husband. There in Israel, she had a relative named Boaz. Ruth happened to be gleaning in Boaz's barley field. Boaz fell in love with Ruth and began to take care of her. This was his blessing to her: "May the Lord, the God of Israel, under whose wings you have come to take refuge, reward you fully."

  This blessing comes to people who seek shelter in God.

Dear God

Thank You for blessing people who seek help from You.

" . . .with all
his might."

Samson put his hands
on the center pillars of the
temple and pushed against
them with all his might.
"Let me die with the
Philistines," he prayed.
And the temple
crashed down.
Judges 16:29–30

Do you have a favorite superhero?
There are so many to choose from—
Superman, Batman, Spiderman, and
Daredevil are just a few. Samson is not
just a superhero. He carried out many
heroic acts for Israel's freedom. God's

Spirit was with him from beginning to end. He tore a lion apart with his bare hands! He killed a thousand men using a donkey's jawbone! He tore the gates off the city of Gaza! By the power of the Spirit, Samson did many amazing things for Israel.

The greatest thing Samson did was the last thing he ever did. Samson's enemies had captured him and cut out his eyes. He was on display like an animal in a zoo. Had his heroic life ended in defeat?

Samson was taken into a temple to entertain his enemies. Three thousand men and women were watching. He put his hands on the pillars that held the roof of the building. "O God, please strengthen me one more time," Samson prayed. Then God enabled him to push over the pillars, and this destroyed the temple. Thousands of enemies died with Samson that day.

Samson did this to show one last time that God was with him. He died for God's people, and this makes him much more than a superhero. Samson is a hero of the faith.

Dear God

Help me to be a hero of the faith like Samson.

"The queen
of Sheba. . ."

When the queen of Sheba
realized how wise Solomon
was, and when she
saw the palace he had built,
she was breathless.
1 Kings 10:4–5

The queen of Sheba was from a far-away land. There she heard of Solomon, the king of Israel, and his wisdom. She came to see him and test him with hard questions. Picture this beautiful woman riding into Jerusalem with a long camel train. The camels carried rare spices, gold, and precious stones as gifts for the king. The queen talked with Solomon about everything on her mind. Solomon answered all her questions.

The queen of Sheba saw Solomon's wisdom. She said to him, "What I heard about you was true. You have great wisdom. I didn't believe it until I came and saw it with my own eyes. Your wisdom is greater than what I was told."

Where did Solomon get his wisdom? He asked God for it. "Give me an understanding mind so that I can govern your people well and know the difference between right and wrong," he prayed.

Anyone can have wisdom. All you need to do is ask for it. The Bible says, "If you need wisdom—if you want to know what God wants you to do—ask him, and he will gladly tell you."

Dear God

Help me to remember that all wisdom comes from You.

"He suffered
from leprosy."

But though Naaman
was a mighty warrior,
he suffered from leprosy.

2 Kings 5:1

This man Naaman was powerful
and desperate. He was the commander
of the Syrian army. He was also a leper.
This means he suffered from an incur-
able disease of the skin called leprosy.
Naaman heard of a prophet in Israel
who could cure him. So he went to
Israel to find Elisha the prophet. When
he found him, he was told to wash in the
Jordan River seven times. This made
Naaman furious.

Naaman was an important man!

He'd come to Israel with all his followers carrying hundreds of pounds of silver and gold. He arrived at Elisha's poor little house expecting more than he got. Naaman expected Elisha to come out of his house. But Elisha's servant came out instead. Naaman wanted Elisha to say some magic words. He expected a sacrifice to God and some soothing ointment for the leprosy. Instead, he was told to wash in the ordinary water of the Jordan River. Naaman was too proud to do this.

The same is true today. People are sick in their souls. They don't have leprosy, but they have sin. And they are too proud for the simple remedy of faith. This cure seems too simple. But it is

God's way. Faith in Jesus is the only cure for sin.

Dear God

Help me not to be prideful.

" . . .a shield
around me."

So many are saying,
"God will never
rescue him!"
But you, O LORD, are a
shield around me,
my glory, and the one
who lifts my head high.
Psalm 3:2–3

This is a song by David, the king of Israel. At the time, his own son, Absalom, was hunting him down. Absalom rebelled against his father. He even tried to kill him and take over the throne of Israel.

Things were so bad for David that

people said not even God could help him. But nothing is impossible for God. He can always help. David found help in God, and so can we.

David said, "O Lord, You are my shield and my glory, the one who lifts my head high." He prayed, crying out loud to the Lord, and he knew that God heard him. His faith made him sure of this. What great hope we have that God hears our prayers!

Prayer gave David real peace. This is why he tells of how soundly he could sleep, despite his troubles. "I lay down and slept," he said. "I woke up in safety, for the Lord was watching over me." David made his requests known to God, and his heart and mind were kept by God's peace.

Dear God

Please give me the same peace King David had by trusting in You.

". . .the glory
of God."

The heavens tell of the glory of God.
The skies display his marvelous craftsmanship.
Day after day they continue to speak;
night after night they make him known.
Psalm 19:1–2

Do you want to know God? Is there someone you love who you hope will believe in God? Here is an easy way to see God. The heavens announce God's glory. The skies shout about the work of His hands.

This has been happening since the fourth day of Creation, when God said, "Let bright lights appear in the sky." Since then, they continue to speak about God day after day. Night after night, they make Him known. If only people would pay attention! It doesn't matter where you are from or what language you speak. Nature tells all about God. Yes, God is invisible. But the Bible says that God and all of His power can be seen through nature.

Many people pray that their family and friends will be open to God. They want them to believe in Jesus Christ. We hope they will hear the gospel. God's Creation is the greatest preacher of all.

Let's pray that everyone will see it and believe it!

Dear God

Help me to open
my eyes every day
to see Your
wonderful Creation.

" . . .watchmen
on your walls."

O Jerusalem, I have posted watchmen on your walls; they will pray to the LORD day and night for the fulfillment of his promises. Take no rest, all you who pray. Give the LORD no rest until he makes Jerusalem the object of praise throughout the earth.

Isaiah 62:6–7

Policemen watch over our towns and cities. They try to make sure that nothing bad happens to us. In ancient Israel, policemen were called watchmen—because the time between sunset and sunrise was divided into three watches. Each watch had different watchmen, so someone had to stay up all night to watch the city and keep it safe from enemies.

The Bible says that God has set watchmen on the walls of Jerusalem. These are not the actual watchmen who kept an eye on Jerusalem—they are Christians who pray. Wouldn't you like to be a watchman like that? They don't shout that enemies are coming—they pray to God until He makes Jerusalem a thing of praise in the earth. That happens when Jesus comes back.

We don't have to be strong or famous to pray like this. Small prayers are important prayers. A person who says to God, "Lord, I love You," has said something very important. Someone who can stop and say, "Thank You," to God has done something very special. You could be that person!

Dear God

Help me to thank You in prayer every day!

". . .from inside
the fish."

Then Jonah prayed to the LORD his God from inside the fish. He said, "I cried out to the LORD in my great trouble, and he answered me."

Jonah 2:1–2

Jonah was a man who ran from God. Do you think he got very far?

God wanted Jonah to go to Nineveh and preach the gospel. Jonah didn't want to do this. Instead, he got on a boat headed away from Nineveh. But a terrible storm blew up, and the ship's crew thought Jonah was to blame. So they tossed Jonah overboard, and a large fish swallowed him. Inside the fish, Jonah prayed to God. God answered, and after three days, the fish spit Jonah out on the shore.

Jonah was a real person with a real story. The Bible uses his story to tell about Jesus. Jesus said, "Jonah was in the belly of the great fish for three days and three nights. . . . I will be in the heart of the earth for three days and three nights." Jonah's experience inside the fish was a sign that pointed to Christ's resurrection from the dead. Jonah could never have known this. He only knew that he had disobeyed God, and so he was swallowed by a fish. But God is the great director of history—Jonah's history and your history, too.

Dear God

Help me to remember that no one can run from You!

" . . .a ruler
of Israel."

But you, O Bethlehem
Ephrathah, are only a
small village in Judah.
Yet a ruler of Israel
will come from you.

Micah 5:2

Bethlehem was a tiny place. Why do you think Jesus was born there? The name Bethlehem means "the house of bread." Jesus is the bread of life. It was in the little town of Bethlehem that the bread of life came to us. That is when Bethlehem became the real house of bread.

The Bible also calls Jesus the Good

Shepherd of the sheep, and we are His sheep. It's interesting that He was born in Bethlehem because it was the town of David. David was a shepherd, too, and later he became the king of Israel.

The night that Jesus was born, shepherds were in the fields outside of Bethlehem. They were guarding their sheep. Suddenly, an angel of the Lord appeared, and they were very afraid. But the angel said, "Don't be afraid! I bring you good news of great joy! The Savior has been born tonight in Bethlehem! Go there and you will find a baby wrapped up and lying in a manger."

Those shepherds went into Bethlehem, the town of King David. There they found Jesus, the Good Shepherd. He was sleeping in a manger. A manger is the place where farmers put food for their sheep and cattle. The Good Shepherd is also spiritual food for His sheep—and we are His sheep!

Dear God

Thank You for sending Jesus to give His sheep the spiritual "food" they need.

"We have seen
his star."

Wise men from eastern lands arrived in Jerusalem, asking, "Where is the newborn king of the Jews? We have seen his star as it arose, and we have come to worship him."

Matthew 2:1–2

When Jesus was born, right away people wanted to know Him. Men from far away asked, "Where is the baby called King of the Jews?" The child was very young. He'd done nothing yet as the Savior of the world. But people were seeking Him already!

God created all the people who live on the earth. There is a reason for this. All people should seek after God. We should reach out for God as if we were blindfolded. He is not far from any of us, and the Bible says that we live and move and exist in God. God can't be seen in a picture on the wall, but through Jesus, He is a living person whom we can know and love.

Long ago, wise men came from far away looking for Jesus, and they found Him. Since then, millions of people have also thirsted for Jesus and found Him. You know what it is like to be thirsty. Your soul is thirsty for God. Seek Jesus. He will be like a drink of water to you,

and your soul will never
be thirsty again!

Dear God

I don't want to
be thirsty
anymore—help
me to always seek
Your son, Jesus!

"They opened
their treasure."

Then they opened their treasure chests and gave him gifts of gold, frankincense, and myrrh.

Matthew 2:11

The wise men were expecting to see a newborn king. What they found was a baby who seemed to be just the son of an ordinary carpenter. Still, they presented to Him their rich gifts of gold, frankincense, and myrrh. These are the first and most famous Christmas presents ever! Do you know why they are so special?

Gold is a gift for a king, that's for sure. In the Bible, gold is used as a symbol for God. And gold doesn't rust.

This shows that God is pure and can't be spoiled. The little boy named Jesus was God.

The priests of Israel used frankincense in worship. It is a reminder that Jesus leads our worship to God.

Myrrh is sap from a plant. People find it by cutting through the bark of a tree. This is like Jesus' experience on the cross when a soldier cut Him with a spear. Myrrh reminds us that Jesus died for our sins.

These three precious gifts show us just who was living in that little Middle Eastern town of Bethlehem. The wise men did not find just an ordinary baby. They found the King of Kings and the very God of the universe!

Dear God

Thank You for Your Son who was so small, yet the mighty God of Creation!

". . .an angel
of the Lord."

That night some shepherds were in the fields outside the village, guarding their flocks of sheep. Suddenly, an angel of the Lord appeared among them.

Luke 2:8–9

I wonder if the shepherds were thinking about God that night. It's possible that they were praying. Or maybe they were sleeping. Suddenly, the glory of the Lord was all around them! Those hardworking men were afraid. An angel tried to calm them down. Then all around them were thousands of angels praising God. "Glory to God in the highest heaven, and peace on earth to all whom God favors," they sang. Imagine how this amazed and scared the shepherds!

These rough shepherds had courage, though. They said to each other, "Let's go to Bethlehem and see this." So they went looking for a baby wrapped in cloths, lying in a manger.

The shepherds found Mary, Joseph, and Jesus in a humble stable because there was no room for them in the inn. The shepherds and everyone they told were amazed at what happened.

Jesus wasn't born in a beautiful palace. He wasn't famous like a movie star. He simply came to do God's work and serve others. He didn't want to be served like a king, even though He is the King of Kings.

Dear God

Help me to be humble like Jesus.

"There is the Lamb of God."

The next day John saw Jesus coming toward him and said, "Look! There is the Lamb of God who takes away the sin of the world!"

John 1:29

Everyone knows that Jesus wasn't really a lamb. He was a man. For His whole life, He wasn't like a lamb at all. He was strong and bold until the end. Then He became like a lamb. The Bible says that when Jesus died, "He was led as a lamb to the slaughter. And as a sheep is silent before the shearers, he did not open his mouth."

In the times of the Old Testament, people made sacrifices to God for their sins. These sacrifices were usually lambs. Year after year, people made these sacrifices. Then Jesus came. He was the last sacrifice for sin. No one has to kill a little lamb again because of sin. Jesus is the Lamb of God whose death took away the sin of the world. "For God so loved the world that he gave his only Son, so that everyone who believes in him will not perish but have eternal life."

Dear God

Thank You for giving Jesus to
be the sacrifice for my sin.

"Fill the jars
with water."

Jesus told the servants, "Fill the jars with water." When the jars had been filled to the brim, he said, "Dip some out and take it to the master of ceremonies."

John 2:7–8

One day, Jesus' mother was a guest at a wedding celebration in a village called Cana. Jesus and His followers were there, too. But the wine ran out before the feast was over. Jesus' mother told Him, "They have no more wine." And she said to the servants, "Do whatever he tells you."

Six stone water pots were there. They were used for Jewish religious ceremonies and held twenty to thirty gallons each. Jesus told the servants, "Fill the jars with water." They filled the jars to the brim.

Then Jesus said, "Dip some out and take it to the man in charge of the feast." The man tasted what he thought was water, but Jesus had turned it to wine!

This was the first miracle Jesus ever did. Why do you think Jesus did this miracle? It was a sign showing who Jesus is. Jesus did miracles like these to show His glory and power and to help people believe in Him.

Dear God

Thank You for miracles that show me Your power.

" . . .unless you
are born again."

Jesus replied, "I assure you, unless you are born again, you can never see the Kingdom of God."
"What do you mean?" exclaimed Nicodemus.
John 3:3–4

When you have a question, don't you think your teacher should have the answer? Nicodemus was a teacher for all of Israel. But when Jesus said, "You have to be born again," Nicodemus didn't know what this meant. Jesus told him that it is difficult to explain. It is like trying to follow the wind. We can hear and feel the wind, but we don't know where it came from or where it is going.

By believing in Jesus, a person has a second birth. This is sometimes called the new birth. When it happens, that person is born again. To see this new birth in a person's life, you must look carefully. It's like the wind—very hard to see.

Have you ever seen fruit hanging from a tree? Sometimes it is hard to see because the leaves hide it. A person who is born again has special fruit in his or her life. Look carefully and you may see love, joy, peace, patience, kindness, goodness, faithfulness, gentleness, and self-control. That is how you know if a person has been born again.

Dear God

I want to please You—
help me to grow all of Your
good fruit in my life.

"And if God
cares. . ."

> "And if God cares so wonderfully for flowers that are here today and gone tomorrow, won't he more surely care for you?"
>
> Matthew 6:30

Think about the rain. It comes down on everything—on roses, poppies, lilies, dandelions, moss, weeds, everything! Why? Because God cares about all these things.

But there are so many things to care about in the universe. Why would God be concerned with flowers? The answer is found in Genesis. It says that when

God made the light, "It was good." Then God made the dry land and the seas. "And God saw that it was good." He grew all kinds of plants on the earth. "And God saw that it was good." Next, God made the sun, moon, and stars. What did God think of this? "And God saw that it was good." Then God made fish and birds. "And God saw that it was good." Then all kinds of animals were made. "And God saw that it was good."

Six times in Genesis, God saw that it was good. This means that God enjoys His Creation. It is delightful to Him. This is why the rain falls on all things. God cares for it all. Since God sends rain on each and every little flower, you

know that He cares
for you, too!

Dear
God

Thank You for caring
about me!

"Please give me
a drink."

Jesus, tired from the long walk, sat wearily beside the well about noontime. Soon a Samaritan woman came to draw water, and Jesus said to her, "Please give me a drink."

John 4:6–7

It was about noon one day, and Jesus was alone, resting by a well. A woman came to the well to draw out some water. Jesus asked her to give Him some. In those days, this wasn't done. Men and women had nothing to do with each other unless they were married. Plus, the woman in this story was a Samaritan. Jesus was a Jew. The Jews thought they were much better than the Samaritans, and so they never spoke to each other.

Most women in those days got their water in the morning. Then they had what they needed for that day. Plus, they didn't have to carry water in the heat of the day. But this woman was an outcast in her village. She had been married several times. The other women stayed away from her because she was a sinner.

You might say this woman had three strikes against her. She was a sinner. She was a Samaritan. She was a woman. To everyone else, she was out, but not to Jesus. This story shows that Jesus came for the outcasts of this world. He came for sinners and poor people. He came for everyone, no matter who they are.

Dear God

Thank You for not playing favorites— You care for everyone.

"And they all ate."

Then Jesus took the loaves,
gave thanks to God,
and passed them out to the
people. Afterward he did
the same with the fish.
And they all ate until
they were full.

John 6:11

Huge crowds sometimes followed Jesus wherever He went. They'd seen His miracles, and they wanted to see more.

On a warm springtime day, Jesus went up into the hills and sat down. His disciples sat around Him. Soon a crowd of people climbed the hill, looking for Him. He asked one of His disciples, "Philip, can we buy bread to feed these people?"

Philip replied, "It would take a small fortune to feed them!"

Then Andrew spoke up. "There's a boy here with five loaves of bread and two fish. But what good is that with this huge crowd?"

"Tell everyone to sit down," Jesus ordered. The crowd sat down on the grassy slope. There were five thousand men and even more women and children. Then Jesus took the loaves, gave thanks to God, and passed them out. Afterward He did the same with the fish.

And they all ate until they were full. "Gather the leftovers," Jesus said, "so that nothing is wasted." Twelve baskets were filled with leftovers!

This miracle caused many people to believe in Jesus. It was a sign to help people understand that Jesus is the bread of life. He came not to feed our body, but to feed our soul.

Dear God

Thank You for feeding not only my body, but my soul, too.

"People need more than bread."

Then the Devil came and said to him, "If you are the Son of God, change these stones into loaves of bread."
But Jesus told him, "No! The Scriptures say, 'People need more than bread for their life; they must feed on every word of God.'"

Matthew 4:3–4

TWO things we cannot live without are food and water. Even Jesus got hungry. But He knew that people needed two kinds of food. There is food for the body and food for the soul. Everyone knows about the food for our body. Jesus came to teach us about the other food. In fact, it was one of the first things He talked about. "People need more than bread for their life," Jesus said. "They must feed on every word of God."

One day Jesus was out in the country-side. Thousands of people came there to see and hear Him. When it came time to eat, no one had any food. With five loaves of bread and two fish, Jesus fed them all. The same people crowded around Jesus the next day. He told them, "You only came here because I fed you yesterday. But God gives you the true bread from heaven."

"Please, give us this bread," they begged.

Jesus answered them, "I am the bread of life. Come to me and you will never be hungry."

No one can go without food. No one should go without knowing that Jesus is the real food.

Dear God

Help me to remember that Jesus is the real Bread of Life.

"Anyone who
listens. . ."

Dear God

I want to make my spiritual house strong—help me to follow the Golden Rule.

"And suddenly
all was calm."

And Jesus answered, "Why are you afraid? You have so little faith!" Then he stood up and rebuked the wind and waves, and suddenly all was calm.

Matthew 8:26

Do you know how to swim? Some of Jesus' followers didn't. One time when they were in a boat on a big lake, the wind began to tip the boat. It was filling with water! They were afraid even though Jesus was in the same boat. He wasn't afraid of the storm. In fact, He was asleep! His followers were afraid because they believed more in the storm than in Jesus. So Jesus scolded them, "You have so little faith!" They believed in the wrong thing.

Many people today believe in the wrong thing. They have little faith in Jesus and great faith in the world. Hard times can come to us in this world. They are like the storm in this story. Jesus may seem to be sleeping through your storm, but you should always believe in Him. Maybe the storm has come to help you believe in Him even more.

Jesus' followers cried out, "Lord, save us!" They did just the right thing. The Bible says, "Anyone who calls on the name of the Lord will be saved."

Dear God

Thank You for saving us
when we have faith in You.

"They were
like sheep."

And wherever he went, he healed people of every sort of disease and illness. He felt great pity for the crowds that came. . . . They were like sheep without a shepherd.

Matthew 9:35–36

Jesus was born in Israel because He was a Jew. He loves all people, but He first came to His own people—the Jews. To God, they are like a flock of sheep. Jesus came to be their shepherd and bring them back to God. The leaders of Israel at the time only took care of themselves. God's sheep had no shepherd.

Long before Jesus came, a man named Ezekiel asked them:

"Shouldn't you shepherds take care of God's people? You have all you need, but you don't take care of the flock. You haven't strengthened the weak, healed the sick, or bandaged the injured. You haven't brought back the stray sheep or searched for the lost. You've ruled Israel harshly and brutally. They were scattered because there was no shepherd. Then they became food for wild animals. My sheep wandered all over the mountains and on every hill. They were scattered over the whole earth, and no one searched or looked for them."

This is why Jesus came. He said, "I have come to seek and save those who are lost." He is the Good Shepherd who loves all people.

Dear God

Thank You for being the Good Shepherd.

" . . .a place
of prayer."

He said, "The Scriptures declare, 'My Temple will be called a place of prayer,' but you have turned it into a den of thieves!"

Matthew 21:13

What if you go to church next Sunday and someone is selling tickets? Someone has opened a bank there and people are lined up to get money. They use the money to pay their way into church. Inside the church, you find strangers selling religious items—decorations, books, and gifts. You can buy a hymnal and a Bible to use for worship.

Cushions and chairs are available for rent. If you don't have one, you must stand. After the service, there are refreshments, but you have to pay for them. What would you do?

Would you do what Jesus did? He once saw salesmen selling animals to people who wanted to worship in the temple. They would use the animals as sacrifices. People couldn't worship unless they paid for an animal. Jesus was angry that God's house had been turned into a place to make money. So He drove out the salesmen and animals and turned over their tables and scattered their coins.

Only Jesus could do this because He

is in charge of the church. You are in charge of your own heart. Like the church, it is also God's house. It is important to keep it clean and pure.

Dear God

Help me to keep my heart pure for You.

" . . . produce
a huge harvest."

"The good soil represents the hearts of those who truly accept God's message and produce a huge harvest—thirty, sixty, or even a hundred times as much as had been planted."

Matthew 13:23

Jesus talked about ordinary things to teach people about God. He didn't try to confuse anyone. He wanted the invisible, spiritual things to be clear so that we could understand them. He also gave ordinary acts spiritual meaning so that our lives could remind us of God.

The parable of the sower is about a farmer planting seed. But this was not a vegetable garden, where seeds are planted one by one. This farmer was in a big field planting wheat. He carried a bag of seed over his shoulder. He dipped his big hand into the seed and tossed the seed onto the land. The seed landed on hard earth, in stony ground, in the weeds, or in good earth.

Later, Jesus explained this story. He said that the ground is your heart and the seed is God's Word. Some hearts are hard. The truth of God can't even start growing there. Hearts with no room for Jesus are like ground filled with stones or weeds.

So you might wonder about your heart. Can the seed of the Word grow there? Simply pray every day that God will soften your heart. Ask the Lord to remove the stones and weeds. The Lord will do this, and then the Word of God can grow in you!

Dear God

Please soften my heart and let Your Word grow in me!

"His face shone
like the sun."

As the men watched,
Jesus' appearance changed
so that his face shone like
the sun, and his clothing
became dazzling white.
Matthew 17:2

Jesus Christ was God who came
to live with us as a man. He looked like
an ordinary man. Everyone knew He
came from a town called Nazareth. This
was just an ordinary place. He was raised
in a carpenter's home with brothers and
sisters. Nearly no one knew that Jesus
was God.

One day, Jesus went with three of

His followers to the top of a mountain. There, Peter, James, and John saw something that no one had seen before. They saw Jesus as God. His face shone like the sun and His body was white light.

Just then, two other men appeared with Jesus. Both of them had lived hundreds of years before. One was Moses, the great leader of Israel. The other was Elijah the prophet. Peter wanted to set up tents to worship Moses, Elijah, and Jesus. But God put a stop to this saying, "This is my beloved Son, and I am fully pleased with him. Listen to him."

This happened so people would know that the old way was past. There was no reason to worship anyone other than Jesus. Moses and Elijah had done their jobs. Now Jesus would finish God's plan.

Dear God

Help me to remember that You alone should be worshiped.

"Yes, I am
the vine."

"Yes, I am the vine; you are the branches. Those who remain in me, and I in them, will produce much fruit. For apart from me you can do nothing."

John 15:5

Have you ever seen a grapevine? Jesus once said that He was like a grapevine. The branches on this vine are all the believers in Jesus. Are the vine and the branches separate? No. Can the branches live without the vine? No. The branches depend on the vine.

Inside of a grapevine, sap flows just

like inside a tree. Just like this sap brings life to the branches, Jesus brings life to us. We aren't just friends of Jesus. We are not doing business with God. When we believe in Jesus, something amazing happens. His life begins to flow to us like sap in a vine. All the Lord asks is that we stay connected to the vine. Then, like branches of a grapevine, we will bear fruit for Him. But our fruit is not grapes. Our fruit is a way of life. In our life we will find the fruits of the Spirit—love, joy, peace, patience, kindness, goodness, faithfulness, gentleness, and self-control.

Dear God

I want to grow good fruit—let Jesus flow through my life!

"Seeing their faith. . ."

So they went up to the roof, took off some tiles, and lowered the sick man down into the crowd, still on his mat, right in front of Jesus. Seeing their faith, Jesus said to the man, "Son, your sins are forgiven."

Luke 5:19–20

One day while Jesus was teaching, some religious leaders were sitting nearby. Such men were always around. They came from every village and from as far away as Jerusalem. Some other men came to where Jesus was teaching, carrying a paralyzed man on a mat. They couldn't push through the crowd to Jesus, so they went up to the roof and opened a hole. They lowered the sick man down into the crowd right in front of Jesus. Jesus said to the man, "Son, your sins are forgiven."

The religious leaders said to each other, "Who does this man think He is? He is mocking God! Only God can forgive sins."

Jesus knew what they were thinking. He asked them, "Is it easier to say, 'Your sins are forgiven' or 'Get up and walk'? I'll prove that I have the power to forgive sins."

Then Jesus said to the paralyzed

man, "Stand up. Take your mat, and go on home. You're healed!" Everyone watched as the man jumped up and went home praising God.

Jesus healed many people in His day. But this was not the reason He came. This story plainly shows why God sent Jesus to us. It was to take care of the problem of sin.

Dear God

Thank You for sending Your son, Jesus, to forgive our sins.

"Now he is found."

"We must celebrate with a feast, for this son of mine was dead and has now returned to life. He was lost, but now he is found."
Luke 15:23–24

A man had two sons. The younger one told his father, "I want my share of your money now, instead of waiting until you die." So the father divided his wealth between his sons.

A few days later, the younger son packed up and took a long vacation. He wasted all of his money and lived a wild life. Then his money ran out, and he began to starve. He got a job feeding pigs, but he was so hungry that even the pigs' food looked good to him.

The son finally came to his senses. "At home, even the servants have food to eat," he said. So he went home to his father.

The father saw his son coming from far away. He was filled with love for his son, and he ran to him and hugged and kissed him. His son said, "Father, I've sinned against you. I shouldn't be called your son anymore." But his father put the finest clothes on him. He put a ring on his finger and sandals on his feet. The whole household celebrated with a feast. "My son was dead and has returned to life," he said with joy. "He was lost. But now he is found."

Jesus told this story to show how much God loves us.

Dear God

Thank You for Your love and forgiveness.

"Praise God,
I'm healed!"

One of them,
when he saw that he
was healed, came back
to Jesus, shouting,
"Praise God, I'm healed!"
He fell face down on the
ground at Jesus' feet,
thanking him for
what he had done.
Luke 17:15–16

Here in the United States we have a holiday we call Thanksgiving. It's a day when we give thanks to God for all we have. Here's a story about thanksgiving:

One day, Jesus was near Samaria. In

a village there, ten lepers stood crying out, "Jesus, have mercy on us!" He looked at them and said, "Go see the priests." And as they went, their leprosy disappeared.

One of them came back to Jesus shouting, "Praise God, I'm healed!" He fell at Jesus' feet, giving thanks.

"Didn't I heal ten men?" Jesus asked. "Where are the other nine?"

Then He said to the man, "Stand up and go. Your faith has made you well."

This story shows that not many people give thanks to God. But the Bible says, "Let your lives overflow with thanksgiving for all he has done."

Remember to thank God for everything.
You'll feel great, and God will be happy.

Dear
God

Help me to
remember to
thank You
for everything!

" . . .a man there
name Zacchaeus."

There was a man there
named Zacchaeus. . . .
He tried to get a look at
Jesus, but he was too short
to see over the crowds.
So he ran ahead and
climbed a sycamore tree
beside the road.
Luke 19:2–4

In our country, many people love celebrities like movie stars and rock stars. These famous people are usually good looking. They are often tall and well dressed. You don't see very many short or ugly celebrities. But God doesn't care what anyone looks like. What matters most to God is your heart. He wants you to love Him and seek Him, just like Zacchaeus did.

Here's how Zacchaeus met the Lord. Jesus was traveling to Jerusalem for the last time. He passed through Jericho, where Zacchaeus lived. Zacchaeus was an important tax collector in town, so he was very rich. He wanted to see Jesus as He passed by. But Zacchaeus was too short to see over the crowds. So he ran ahead and climbed a sycamore tree beside the road. He could watch from there.

Zacchaeus probably looked silly in that tree. He was a grown man and a rich man, too. But he didn't care what people thought of him. He just wanted to see Jesus. When Jesus came by, He saw Zacchaeus in the tree and called him by name. "Zacchaeus!" He said. "Quick, come down! I want to stay in your home today."

Of all the people crowding the street that day, Jesus saw Zacchaeus. Why? Because Zacchaeus so badly wanted to see the Lord.

Dear God

I want to be like Zacchaeus—
help me always to look for You!

" . . . walking
on the water."

About three o'clock
in the morning Jesus
came to them,
walking on the water.
Matthew 14:25

Jesus' followers were once taught
a lesson on how to trust the Lord.

One day, Jesus was alone on a
mountain praying. Some of His followers were in a boat, rowing across a huge
lake. Nighttime came, and the boat was
far away from land. They were having
trouble rowing because of strong winds.
Jesus came to help them late at night.
He was walking on the water! The disciples saw Him and screamed. They

thought Jesus was a ghost.

Jesus said, "It's all right. I'm here! Don't be afraid."

Peter, one of the men in the boat, called out, "Lord, if it's You, tell me to come to You by walking on water."

"Come on," Jesus said.

Peter went over the side of the boat and walked on the water toward Jesus! But then he looked around at the high waves and was terrified. As soon as Peter took his eyes off Jesus, he began to sink. He shouted, "Save me, Lord!"

Jesus reached out and grabbed Peter. "You don't have much faith," Jesus said. "Why did you doubt me?" They climbed back into the boat, and the wind stopped.

Peter lost faith for a simple reason. Instead of looking at Jesus, he looked at the waves. We must never stop looking to Jesus, or we might sink, too!

Dear God

Help me to keep my eyes on You and Your son, Jesus Christ.

" . . .everything
she has."

Then a poor widow came and dropped in two pennies. [Jesus] called his disciples to him and said, "I assure you, this poor widow has given more than all the others have given. For they gave a tiny part of their surplus, but she, poor as she is, has given everything she has."

Mark 12:42–44

In the ancient temple, money was collected to give to the poor. This poor widow who gave all her money at the temple is like another widow in the Bible.

The prophet Elijah went to a town called Zarephath. There he saw a widow gathering sticks. He asked her, "Would you bring me a cup of water and a bite of bread?"

"I'll tell you the truth," she answered. "I have no bread in my house. I do have a handful of flour left in the jar and a little cooking oil in the bottom of the jug. I was gathering a few sticks to cook my last meal. Then my son and I will die."

Elijah told her, "Don't be afraid. Cook your meal, but first bake a loaf of bread for me. There will be enough food for you. The Lord tells me you will have flour and oil left over."

The widow did this, and she, Elijah, and her son ate for many days. No matter how much flour and oil they used, there was always enough left over.

These two widows teach us to not be afraid to give to others. When we do, God will take care of everything we need.

Dear God

Help me to give to others as the widow and her son did.

" . . .a beautiful jar."

During supper, a woman
came in with a beautiful jar
of expensive perfume.
She broke the seal and
poured the perfume
over his head.

Mark 14:3

Have you ever wondered if you
should believe in Jesus? Here is a story
about a woman who believed in Jesus
and gave all she had to Him.

Jesus was in Bethany at the home of
Simon the Leper. During supper, a
woman came in with a beautiful jar of
expensive perfume. She opened it and

poured the perfume over Jesus' head. Some of those eating with Him were angry. "What a waste!" they said. "She could have sold that perfume for a small fortune. The money should have gone to the poor!" Then they scolded the woman.

"Leave her alone," said Jesus. "Why scold her for doing a good thing to Me? You will always have the poor to take care of. You can help them whenever you want to. But I won't be with you much longer. She's done what she could and has prepared My body for burial early. Believe Me, wherever the gospel is preached, what this woman has done will be remembered."

It is never a waste to give yourself to Jesus.

Dear God

Help me to give all that I have to You.

"They shouted,
'Praise God!' "

The next day, the news that Jesus was on the way to Jerusalem swept through the city. A huge crowd of Passover visitors took palm branches and went down the road to meet him. They shouted, "Praise God!"

John 12:12–13

This is the beginning of the last week of Jesus' life on the earth.

He and His followers were in a town called Bethphage, near Jerusalem. "Go into the village over there," He told two of His followers. "You'll see a donkey there, with its colt beside it. Untie them and bring them here."

The two did as Jesus said and brought the donkeys to Him. They threw their coats over the little colt, and Jesus sat on it and rode into Jerusalem.

When Jesus was born, He was called the King of the Jews. You'd think He would ride into the city on a beautiful, tall horse. After all, He was the King! Instead, He rode on a baby donkey.

Hundreds of years before, a man predicted this would happen. He wrote, "Tell the people of Israel, 'Look, your King is coming to you. He is humble, riding on a donkey—even on a donkey's colt.' "

A crowd was waiting for Jesus in Jerusalem. They spread their coats on the road ahead of Him. Others cut branches from the trees and spread them on the road. The crowds all around Him shouted, "Praise God for the Son of David! Praise God in highest heaven!"

Dear God

Thank You so much for Your son, Jesus Christ, and all He has done!

". . .on ahead
to pray."

Then Jesus brought them
to an olive grove called
Gethsemane, and he said,
"Sit here while I go
on ahead to pray."
Matthew 26:36

Jesus often took His followers to rest and pray in the Garden of Gethsemane. They were there praying on the night before Jesus died. The days before this night had made Jesus very tired. But the next day would be the hardest day of His life—the day He died. He was so weary that an angel came from heaven to help Him.

You may have heard people talk of angels or seen pictures of angels. They don't often show up in Bible stories. Angels appear only when something very important is happening in God's plan. The most important thing that ever happened was Jesus' life. Angels were there right from the beginning. An angel told both Mary and Joseph about Jesus' birth.

Jesus once spent forty days alone in the wilderness. There, He didn't eat, but He prayed. When this time was over, angels came to help Him. The next time angels appeared was here in Gethsemane. Angels were there when Jesus came back to life, too. There was an earthquake when an angel came to Jesus' grave. The Bible says this angel looked like lightning and his clothes were white as snow.

We shouldn't expect angels to appear again until Jesus comes back. Then, Jesus said, "I will come in the glory of my Father with his angels."

Dear God

Help me to focus only on You and Your son—and nothing else.

" . . . with me
in paradise."

Then he said, "Jesus, remember me when you come into your Kingdom." And Jesus replied, "I assure you, today you will be with me in paradise."

Luke 23:42–43

IT is never too late to believe in Jesus. When Jesus died, two criminals were crucified with Him. Each one hung on a cross. One was on Jesus' right side, the other on His left.

One of the criminals made fun of the Lord. "So you're the Messiah, are you?" he sneered. "Prove it! Save yourself, and save us, too."

But the other criminal didn't like this. "You're dying," he said to the mocking criminal. "Don't you fear God even now? We did evil things and deserve to die. But this man hasn't done anything wrong." Then he said, "Jesus, remember me when you come into your Kingdom." Jesus replied, "I promise you, today you will be with me in paradise."

The criminal died that day. The last thing he did was to believe in Jesus, and now he is in paradise with Him!

Dear God

Thank You for accepting
anyone who believes on You,
no matter when.

"Receive the
Holy Spirit."

He spoke to them again and said, "Peace be with you. As the Father has sent me, so I send you." Then he breathed on them and said to them, "Receive the Holy Spirit."

John 20:21–22

Jesus' followers were afraid, confused, and very sad. They'd spent three years with Jesus, but suddenly He was gone. He'd been arrested and killed in a horrible way. They were afraid that they would be arrested, too. They were confused about what had happened and what to do next. And they were so sad that Jesus had died.

The followers were in a secret meeting two days after Jesus died. All the doors were closed for fear of the religious leaders. But all of a sudden Jesus stood with them saying, "Peace be with you."

Jesus' followers were overjoyed when they saw Him. Again, He said, "Peace be with you." He didn't want them to be afraid of the religious leaders. He also didn't want them to be afraid of Him. This was the first time they'd seen Jesus back to life.

Next, Jesus did the most wonderful thing imaginable. He breathed on them and said, "Receive the Holy Spirit."

And so they did. From that day on, they were different because they had the Spirit of God inside them. He said, "I am with you always, even to the end of the age." As the Spirit, Jesus made His promise true.

Dear God

Thank You for sending the Holy Spirit to live inside all believers.

"Who are you,
Lord?"

"Who are you, Lord?"
Saul asked. "I am Jesus,
whom you are persecuting,"
he replied.

Acts 9:5 NIV

The man who asked this question was changed forever. If everyone would ask God, "Who are you, Lord?" the world would be a better place.

The man who asked this question was named Paul. He was born about the same time Jesus was, across the sea from Israel. Paul was sent to Jerusalem to study the religious law of the Jews. As a young man, he was well known by Israel's priests and elders. Paul was a rising star in Jerusalem.

One day, God knocked Paul to the ground and spoke to him. This is when Paul asked, "Who are you, Lord?" God's answer changed him.

The Lord didn't say, "I am the God of your fathers." Paul may have expected him to say, "I am the God of Abraham, Isaac, and Jacob." Rather than this, the Lord said, "I am Jesus of Nazareth."

Paul asked, "Who are you, Lord?" and found that Jesus Christ is God.

"Who are you, Lord?" is a powerful prayer, and God is happy to answer, "I am Jesus Christ."

Dear God

Thank You for making it plain
who You are—You and Jesus
are the same.

"Full of love
and kindness. . ."

You know how full of love
and kindness our Lord Jesus
Christ was. Though he was
very rich, yet for your sakes
he became poor, so that
by his poverty he could
make you rich.

2 Corinthians 8:9

Every king has a crown. Most
crowns are made of gold and precious
jewels, but Jesus Christ's crown was
made of thorns. We try to rid our
world of thorns. We chop, burn, gather,
and dump them. But weeds, brambles,
and choking vines return to our land

year after year. Tumbleweeds line our fences no matter how hard we try to destroy them.

Rock miners didn't have to dig to find the material for Christ's crown. Jewelers didn't have to cut and polish gems to decorate His head. The Bible says, "They made a crown of long, sharp thorns and put it on his head, and they placed a stick in his right hand as a scepter. Then they knelt before Him in mockery, yelling, "Hail! King of the Jews!"

Long before this, God told Adam and Eve, "I have cursed the ground. It will grow thorns for you."

Today we still have thorns growing

all around. We can't get rid of them. But our curse became Christ's crown, and He saved us from our sins.

Dear God

Thank You for bearing our crown of thorns by sending Jesus to save us.

". . .the peace that comes from Christ."

And let the peace that comes from Christ rule in your hearts. For as members of one body you are all called to live in peace. And always be thankful.

Colossians 3:15

Jesus said, "I am leaving you with a gift—peace of mind and heart. And the peace I give isn't like the peace the world gives. So don't be troubled or afraid."

Ever since the times of Jesus, peace has been compared with a dove. This bird is also a symbol of the Holy Spirit.

When the Spirit came down upon Jesus, it looked like a dove. The Holy Spirit gives us God's peace.

Because Christians have God's Spirit, we don't worry about anything. Instead, we pray about everything. In prayer, we tell God what we need, and we thank Him for all things. This brings us God's peace. This peace is impossible to explain. It is far more wonderful than your mind can understand. Let this peace guard your heart and mind as you live in Christ.

Doves are very shy. It is easy to scare them away. This is true with peace, too. It can come and go like a bird. One day, Jesus will bring His peace to the earth to stay forever. He will bring the kingdom of peace.

Dear God

I thank You that one day You'll bring peace to the earth.

" . . .as white as snow."

His head and his hair
were white like wool,
as white as snow.
And his eyes were bright
like flames of fire.
Revelation 1:14

No one today really knows what Jesus looked like. But one old man described him in the Bible. John, who lived on a little island called Patmos about sixty-five years after Jesus died, had a vision of the Lord. He saw the resurrected Jesus.

John was praying on a Sunday when he heard a voice behind him—it turned out to be Jesus Christ. John wrote that Jesus was wearing a long robe with a gold sash across His chest. His hair was woolly, as white as snow. His eyes flashed like fire. His feet were like pure, shining bronze. His voice thundered like ocean waves that break on the shore. Seven stars were in His right hand, and a sharp sword came out of His mouth. His face was as bright as the sun on a perfectly clear day.

When John saw Jesus, he fainted. But Jesus said, "Don't be afraid! I am the first, the last, and the living one. I was dead, and look, I'm alive forever and ever!"

Think of that! Jesus is alive right

now. He is holding and loving us like those seven bright stars in His hand.

Dear God

Thank You for being our wonderful and living Lord!

". . .a new heaven
and a new earth."

Then I saw a new heaven
and a new earth. . . .
And I saw the holy city,
the new Jerusalem,
coming down from God
out of heaven.
Revelation 21:1–2

Do you know how the Bible ends? In the end, heaven comes to earth. John saw this in his vision. It is a holy city named the New Jerusalem. It will come down out of heaven from God. This city is like a beautiful bride who is ready to marry her husband.

John heard a voice coming from

God's throne. "Look," the voice said. "The home of God is now among people! He will live with them. They will be His people. God will be with them. All their tears will be wiped away. There will be no more death, sorrow, crying, or pain. The old world is gone forever."

Then the one sitting on the throne said, "Look, I am making everything new!"

This wonderful city of God is the hope of every Christian. We will all be there living with God on the new earth. This is God's promise: "It is finished! I'm the Alpha and the Omega—the beginning and the end. I will freely give the thirsty people water from the spring of the water of life. I'll be their God and they'll be My children."

Dear God

Thank You for Your glory that lasts forever and ever!

" . . .a tree
of life."

And the angel showed me
a pure river with the water
of life, clear as crystal,
flowing from the throne of
God and of the Lamb,
coursing down the center
of the main street.
On each side of the river
grew a tree of life.
Revelation 22:1–2

Do you remember the first two chapters of the Bible? They tell the story of
God's creation of the heavens, the earth,
and all things. Adam and Eve were there
living in a perfect garden in Eden. There

was a river and the tree of life. These two chapters of the Bible tell of God's paradise. God was everything to the people who lived there. They loved and lived by God, and God loved them. Together they walked through the garden in the cool of the day.

Do you remember the third chapter of the Bible? In it, the man and woman were tempted away from God. Suddenly paradise was gone. They were cut off from the tree of life and lost everything. Then the Bible begins to tell the story of how God brings men and women back to Himself—back to paradise. This story runs for 1,885 chapters of sixty-six books of the Bible, which contain thirty-one thousand verses! Finally the book of life is opened, and hell and death are thrown into the lake of fire.

Then come the last two chapters of the Bible. Here again is paradise, which is watered by the river of life. Here again is the tree of life. Here we love and live with God forever!

Dear God

Thank You for all You have done, what You are doing, and what You will do!

Daniel Partner is a veteran Christian author and editor who lives in Oregon. His books include *The Wonder of Christmas*, *All Things Are Possible*, *Women of Sacred Song* (written with his wife, Margaret), and *The One-Year Book of Poetry* (coedited with Philip Comfort). All are available at Christian bookstores nationwide.

Besides his publishing work, Daniel is active in preserving and performing mid-nineteenth-century American popular music. He can be contacted by e-mail at author@danpartner.com.